kebabs
& other light grills

kebabs
& other light grills

Ghillie Başan

photography by Richard Jung

RYLAND
PETERS
& SMALL

LONDON NEW YORK

Dedication
For Nina. Even you can cook with this book!

Senior Designer Sonya Nathoo
Senior Commissioning Editor Julia Charles
Photographic Art Direction Megan Smith
Production Controller Toby Marshall
Art Director Leslie Harrington
Publishing Director Alison Starling

Prop Stylist Róisín Nield
Food Stylist Sunil Vijayaker
Indexer Hilary Bird

First published in 2010 by Ryland Peters & Small
20–21 Jockey's Fields, London WC1R 4BW
www.rylandpeters.com

10 9 8 7 6 5 4 3 2 1

Text © Ghillie Başan 2010
Design and photographs © Ryland Peters & Small 2010

ISBN: 978-1-84597-973-7

Printed and bound in China

Author's acknowledgements
As always, I have many people to thank on my travels,
but the book itself would never have come about without the
support of my editor, Julia Charles, who is always a delight
to work with. My thanks also go to Richard, Megan, Sonya,
Ròisìn and Sunil, for making this book look so appetizing.

Contents

Introduction

The story of the kebab and its Southeast Asian cousin, the satay, is really a very old one as it can be traced back to the early travellers, hunters and nomadic peoples who would set up fires to ward off wild animals and provide warmth as well as to roast a whole beast, but the invention of skewering small cuts of meat onto sticks and metal swords is much more recent and its origins can be attributed to the Persians and Arabs of the Middle Ages. Now known universally as the 'kebab' or 'kabob', this traditional method spread with Islamic Empire across the Middle East, North Africa, India and Pakistan and later made an impact on the cultures of Indo-China where the method became known as 'satay'.

Originally, kebabs were invented as a way of using up poor cuts of meat, often marinated with spices to tenderize and disguise any flaws, but the method rendered the meat so tasty that kebab houses and satay stalls became features of their respective culinary landscape. In the Middle East and North Africa the kebab is generally the main part of a meal and therefore may be served on its own with lemon to squeeze over it, whereas the satay dishes of Southeast Asia are often served as snacks or as part of a banquet and are invariably accompanied by a fiery relish or a dipping sauce.

The key to all kebabs is the marinating and basting to render the meat or fish tender, tasty and juicy. Skewers are also an important feature. Most meat kebabs are cooked and served on metal skewers, which retain a higher heat and cook the inside of the meat; vegetable and fish kebabs are often cooked on wooden skewers, some of which can enhance the flavour, such as cherry, juniper and birch; and satay dishes are often prepared on wooden or bamboo skewers, which need to be soaked in water before use, although some local specialities thread the ingredients onto stalks of sugar cane or lemongrass for flavour and effect. Light and delicious, cooked over charcoal or under conventional grills, kebabs are simple and versatile food for any time of the year.

meat

For the kebabs:

500 g finely minced lean lamb

1 onion, grated

2 teaspoons ground cumin

1 teaspoon ground coriander

1 teaspoon paprika

½–1 teaspoon cayenne pepper

1 teaspoon sea salt

a small bunch of fresh flat leaf parsley, finely chopped

a small bunch of fresh coriander, finely chopped

For the hot houmous:

225 g dried chickpeas, soaked overnight and cooked in plenty of water until tender, or a 410-g tin cooked chickpeas, drained

50 ml olive oil

freshly squeezed juice of 1 lemon

1 teaspoon cumin seeds

2 tablespoons light tahini

4 tablespoons thick, strained natural yoghurt

sea salt and freshly ground black pepper

40 g butter

To serve:

a leafy herb salad

flatbreads

2 metal skewers with wide, flat blades

Serves 4–6

Cumin-flavoured lamb kebabs with hot houmous

Typical fodder at the street grills or kebab houses, these kebabs are enjoyed throughout the Middle East and North Africa. To prepare them successfully, you will need large metal skewers with wide, flat blades to hold the meat, which acts like a sheath to the sword.

Mix the minced lamb with the other ingredients and knead well. Pound the meat to a smooth consistency in a large mortar and pestle, or whizz in a food processor. Leave to sit for an hour to let the flavours mingle.

Meanwhile, make the houmous. Preheat the oven to 200°C (400°F) Gas 6. In a food processor, whizz the chickpeas with the olive oil, lemon juice, cumin seeds, tahini and yoghurt. Season to taste, tip the mixture into an ovenproof dish, cover with foil and put in the preheated oven to warm through.

Wet your hands to make the meat mixture easier to handle. Mould portions of the mixture around the skewers, squeezing and flattening it, so it looks like the sheath to the sword.

Prepare a charcoal or conventional grill. Cook the kebabs for 4–5 minutes on each side. Quickly melt the butter and pour it over the houmous. When the kebabs are cooked on both sides, slip the meat off the skewers, cut into bite-sized pieces and serve with the hot houmous on the side with a leafy herb salad and flatbreads.

For the kebab:

500 g minced lean lamb

2 onions, finely chopped

1 fresh green chilli, finely chopped

4 garlic cloves, crushed

1 teaspoon paprika

1 teaspoon ground sumac
(see note on page 38)

leaves from a small bunch of fresh
flat leaf parsley, finely chopped

For the sauce:

2 tablespoons olive oil plus
a knob of butter

1 onion, finely chopped

2 garlic cloves, finely chopped

1 fresh green chilli, deseeded
and finely chopped

1 teaspoon sugar

400-g tin chopped tomatoes

sea salt and freshly ground
black pepper

To serve:

2 tablespoons butter

8 plum tomatoes

1 large pide or plain naan bread,
cut into pieces

1 teaspoon ground sumac

1 teaspoon dried oregano

225 g thick natural yoghurt

a bunch of fresh flat leaf parsley,
chopped

*1 large metal skewer with a wide,
flat blade, plus 1 long thin skewer*

Serves 4

Lamb shish kebab
with yoghurt and flatbread

To my mind this is the ultimate kebab! There are variations throughout the Middle East but this tasty Turkish version, designed to use up day-old 'pide' bread, is outstanding.

Put the minced lamb in a bowl. Add all the other kebab ingredients and knead well, until it resembles a smooth paste and is quite sticky. Cover and chill in the refrigerator for about 15 minutes.

To make the sauce, heat the oil and butter in a heavy-based saucepan. Add the onion, garlic and chilli, and stir until they begin to colour. Add the sugar and tomatoes and cook, uncovered, until quite thick and saucey. Season to taste. Keep warm.

Wet your hands to make the meat mixture easier to handle. Mould portions of the mixture around the skewer, squeezing and flattening it, so it looks like the sheath to the sword. Thread the tomatoes onto the thin skewer.

Prepare a charcoal or conventional grill. Cook the kebab for 4–5 minutes on each side. Add the tomatoes to the grill and cook until charred and soft. While both are cooking, melt the butter in a heavy-based frying pan, add the pide pieces and toss until golden. Sprinkle with some of the sumac and oregano and arrange on a serving plate. Spoon some sauce and half the yoghurt on top.

When the kebab is cooked on both sides, slip the meat off the skewer, cut into pieces and arrange on top of the pide along with the tomatoes. Sprinkle with salt and the remaining sumac and oregano. Add the sauce and yoghurt and garnish with parsley.

For the satay:

500 g pork fillet, cut into bite-sized cubes or strips

For the marinade:

4 shallots, peeled and chopped

4 garlic cloves, peeled

2–3 teaspoons Indian curry powder

2 tablespoons dark soy sauce

2 tablespoons sesame or peanut oil

For the pineapple sauce:

4 shallots, peeled and chopped

2 garlic cloves, chopped

4 dried red chillies, soaked in warm water until soft, deseeded and chopped

1 lemongrass stalk, trimmed and chopped

25 g fresh ginger, peeled and chopped

2 tablespoons sesame or peanut oil

200 ml coconut milk

2 teaspoons tamarind paste (see note on page 37)

2 teaspoons sugar

1 small fresh pineapple, peeled, cored and cut into slices

sea salt

To serve:

Rice Pilaf (see page 61), optional

a packet of short wooden or bamboo skewers, soaked in water before use

Serves 4

Curried pork satay
with pineapple sauce

This spicy satay is popular in Malaysia and Singapore. A combination of Indian, Malay and Chinese traditions, it is best accompanied by a rice pilaf or chunks of bread.

To make the marinade, use a mortar and pestle, or a food processor, to pound the shallots and garlic to form a paste. Stir in the curry powder and soy sauce, and bind with the oil. Rub the marinade into the meat, making sure it is well coated. Cover and refrigerate for at least 2 hours.

In the meantime, prepare the sauce. Using a mortar and pestle, or a food processor, pound the shallots, garlic, chillies, lemongrass and ginger to form a paste. Heat the oil in a heavy-based pan and stir in the paste. Cook for 2–3 minutes until fragrant and beginning to colour, then stir in the coconut milk, tamarind and sugar. Bring the mixture to the boil, then reduce the heat and simmer for about 5 minutes. Season to taste and leave to cool. Using a mortar and pestle, or a food processor, crush 3 slices of the fresh pineapple and beat them into the sauce.

Prepare a charcoal or conventional grill. Thread the marinated meat onto the prepared skewers. Line them up over the hot charcoal or on the grill pan and place the remaining slices of pineapple beside them. Char the pineapple slices and chop them into chunks. Grill the meat until just cooked, roughly 2–3 minutes each side, and serve immediately with the charred pineapple chunks for spearing, and the sauce for dipping.

Fiery beef satay in peanut sauce

For the satay:

500 g beef sirloin, sliced against
the grain into bite-sized pieces

1 tablespoon peanut oil

For the peanut sauce:

60 ml peanut or vegetable oil

4–5 garlic cloves, crushed

4–5 dried serrano chillies,
deseeded and ground with
a pestle and mortar

1–2 teaspoons curry powder

60 g roasted peanuts, finely ground

To serve:

a small bunch of fresh coriander

a small bunch of fresh mint

lime wedges

*a packet of short wooden or
bamboos skewers, soaked in
water before use*

Serves 4–6

Beef, pork or chicken satays cooked in, or served with, a fiery peanut sauce are hugely popular throughout Southeast Asia. This particular sauce is a great favourite in Thailand, Vietnam and Indonesia. It is best to make your own but commercial brands are available under the banner satay or sate sauce.

To make the sauce, heat the oil in a heavy-based saucepan and stir in the garlic until it begins to colour. Add the chillies, curry powder and the peanuts and stir over a gentle heat, until the mixture forms a paste. Remove from the heat and leave to cool.

Put the beef pieces in a bowl. Beat the peanut oil into the sauce and tip the mixture onto the beef. Mix well, so that the beef is evenly coated and thread the meat onto the prepared skewers.

Prepare a charcoal or conventional grill. Cook the satays for 2–3 minutes on each side, then serve the skewered meat with the fresh herbs to wrap around each tasty morsel.

For the sweet and sour sauce:

2 teaspoons peanut oil

1 garlic clove, finely chopped

1 fresh red chilli, deseeded and finely chopped

2 tablespoons roasted peanuts, finely chopped

1 tablespoon Thai fish sauce

2 tablespoons rice wine vinegar

2 tablespoons hoisin sauce

4 tablespoons coconut milk

1–2 teaspoons sugar, to taste

a pinch of sea salt

For the kofta (meatballs):

2 teaspoons peanut or sesame oil

4 shallots, finely chopped

2 garlic cloves, finely chopped

450 g minced pork

2 tablespoons Thai fish sauce

2 teaspoons five-spice powder

2 teaspoons sugar

2 handfuls of fresh white or brown breadcrumbs

sea salt and freshly ground black pepper

To serve:

Simple Noodles (see page 61)

a small bunch of fresh coriander

a packet of short wooden or bamboo skewers, soaked in water before use

Serves 4

Pork kofta kebabs
with sweet and sour sauce

These Asian-style meatball kebabs are best served with a hot, spicy dipping sauce and noodles. The sweet hoisin sauce is available in larger supermarkets and Asian markets.

To make the sauce, heat the oil in a small wok or heavy-based frying pan. Stir in the garlic and chilli and, when they begin to colour, add the peanuts. Stir for a few minutes until the natural oil from the peanuts begins to weep. Add all the remaining ingredients (except the sugar and salt) along with 100 ml water. Let the mixture bubble up for 1 minute. Adjust the sweetness and seasoning to taste with sugar and some salt and set aside.

To make the meatballs, heat the oil in a wok or a heavy-based frying pan. Add the shallots and garlic – when they begin to brown, turn off the heat and leave to cool. Put the minced pork into a bowl, tip in the stir-fried shallot and garlic, fish sauce, five-spice powder and sugar and season with a little salt and lots of pepper. Using your hands, knead the mixture so it is well combined. Cover and chill in the refrigerator for 2–3 hours. Knead the mixture again then tip in the breadcrumbs. Knead well to bind. Divide the mixture into roughly 20 portions and roll into balls. Thread them onto the prepared skewers. Prepare a charcoal or conventional grill. Cook the kebabs for 3–4 minutes on each side, turning them from time to time, until browned.

Reheat the sauce. Serve the kofta with noodles and the hot sweet and sour sauce on the side for dipping.

Spicy beef and coconut kofta kebabs

For the kofta (meatballs):

1 teaspoon coriander seeds

1 teaspoon cumin seeds

175 g desiccated or freshly grated coconut

1 tablespoon coconut oil

4 shallots, peeled and finely chopped

2 garlic cloves, finely chopped

1–2 fresh red chillies, deseeded and finely chopped

350 g lean minced beef

1 beaten egg, to bind

sea salt and freshly ground black pepper

To serve:

2–3 tablespoons freshly grated or desiccated coconut

lime wedges

a packet of short wooden or bamboo skewers, soaked in water before use

Serves 4

Variations of this Asian dish can be found at street stalls from Sri Lanka to the Philippines and South Africa to the West Indies. Simple and tasty, the kofta are delicious served with wedges of fresh lime or a dipping sauce of your choice.

In a small heavy-based frying pan, dry roast the coriander and cumin seeds until they give off a nutty aroma. Using a mortar and pestle, or a spice grinder, grind the roasted seeds to a powder.

In the same pan, dry roast the coconut until it begins to colour and give off a nutty aroma. Tip it onto a plate to cool.

Heat the coconut oil in the same small heavy-based pan and stir in the shallots, garlic and chillies, until fragrant and beginning to colour. Tip them onto a plate to cool.

Put the minced beef in a bowl and add the ground spices, toasted coconut and shallot mixture. Season with salt and pepper and use a fork to mix all the ingredients together, adding a little egg to bind it (you may not need it all). Knead the mixture with your hands and mould it into little balls. Thread the balls onto the prepared skewers.

Prepare a charcoal or conventional grill. Cook the kebabs for 2–3 minutes on each side. Sprinkle the cooked kofta with the toasted coconut and serve with the wedges of lime to squeeze over them.

Lamb and porcini kebabs with sage and parmesan

450 g tender lamb, from the leg or shoulder, cut into bite-sized chunks

4–8 fresh medium-sized porcini, cut into quarters or thickly sliced

2 tablespoons olive oil

freshly squeezed juice of 1–2 lemons

leaves from a bunch of fresh sage, finely chopped (reserve a few whole leaves)

2 garlic cloves, crushed

sea salt and freshly ground black pepper

To serve:

truffle oil, to drizzle

Parmesan shavings

grilled or toasted sourdough bread

4 long, thin metal skewers

Serves 4

Rural feasts in Italy often involve grilling and roasting outdoors. One of the most exciting times is the mushroom season when entire villages hunt for wild mushrooms and gather together to cook them. These kebabs are prepared with freshly picked porcini, but you could substitute them with dried porcini reconstituted in water or field mushrooms.

Put the lamb pieces in a bowl and toss in half the oil and lemon juice. Add the sage and garlic and season with salt and pepper. Cover and leave to marinate for about 2 hours.

Thread the lamb onto skewers adding a quarter, or slice, of porcini every so often with a sage leaf. Brush with any of the marinade left in the bowl. Prepare a charcoal or conventional grill. Cook the kebabs for 3–4 minutes on each side.

Serve immediately with a drizzle of truffle oil and Parmesan shavings and toasted sourdough bread, if liked.

Harissa chicken kebabs
with oranges and preserved lemon

16–20 chicken wings

4 oranges (blood oranges if available), cut into quarters

about 30 g icing sugar

½ a preserved lemon*, finely shredded or chopped

a small bunch of fresh coriander, chopped

For the marinade:

4 tablespoons harissa paste (see note on page 54)

2 tablespoons olive oil

sea salt

4 long, thin metal skewers

Serves 4

With a taste of North Africa, this recipe is quick and easy and best eaten with fingers. The oranges are there to suck on after an explosion of fire on the tongue. They can be cooked separately, or threaded alternately on metal skewers.

Mix the harissa with the olive oil to form a looser paste and add a little salt. Brush the oily mixture over the chicken wings, so that they're well coated. Leave to marinate for 2 hours.

Thread the marinated chicken wings onto the skewers. Prepare a charcoal or conventional grill. Cook on both sides for about 5 minutes. Once the wings begin to cook, dip the orange quarters lightly in icing sugar, thread them onto skewers and grill them for a few minutes, checking that they are slightly charred but not burnt.

Serve the chicken wings and oranges together and scatter the preserved lemon and coriander over the top.

*Note Preserved lemons are used extensively in North African cooking and are whole lemons packed in jars with salt. The interesting thing is that you eat only the rind, which contains the essential flavour of the lemon. They are available from supermarkets and online retailers.

poultry

Lemon chicken kebabs
wrapped in aubergine

freshly squeezed juice of
  2–3 lemons

2 garlic cloves, crushed

4–6 allspice berries, crushed

1 tablespoon crushed dried
  sage leaves

8 chicken thighs, boned
  and skinned

4 aubergines

sunflower oil, for deep-frying

1 tablespoon butter

To serve:

lemon wedges, to serve

salad of your choice

Rice Pilaf (see page 61)

*4 metal or wooden skewers
  (optional)*

an ovenproof dish, well greased

Serves 4

This Ottoman dish is impressive and tasty and best served
with a refreshing salad, such as tomato and cucumber, or
parsley, pepper and onion, and a buttery rice pilaf.

Preheat the oven to 180°C (350°F) Gas 4.

In a shallow bowl, mix together the lemon juice, garlic, allspice berries
and sage leaves. Toss the chicken thighs in the mixture, rolling them
over in the juice, and let marinate for about 2 hours.

Peel the aubergines in strips and slice them thinly lengthways, so that
you have at least 16 long strips. Soak the strips in a bowl of cold, salted
water for about 30 minutes. Drain them and squeeze out the excess
water. In a wok or frying pan, heat sufficient oil for deep-frying and fry
the aubergine in batches, until golden brown. Drain on kitchen paper.

On a board or plate, lay two aubergine strips, one over the other in
a cross, then place a marinated chicken thigh in the middle. Pull the
aubergine strips over the thigh to form a neat parcel. Place the
aubergine parcel, seam-side down, in the prepared ovenproof dish
and repeat the process with the remaining thighs. Pour the rest of the
marinade over the top and dab each parcel with butter. Cover the dish
with foil and cook in the preheated oven for 30 minutes. Remove the
foil, baste the chicken parcels with the cooking juices, and return to the
oven for a further 10 minutes. Serve immediately, threaded onto
skewers to secure them (if using), with wedges of lemon on the side
for squeezing and a salad and rice pilaf.

1 kg chicken breasts, cut into bite-sized pieces

2 tablespoons ghee or butter, melted

For the marinade:

3 fresh red or green chillies, deseeded and chopped

2–3 garlic cloves, chopped

25 g fresh ginger, peeled and chopped

2 tablespoons double cream

3 tablespoons vegetable oil

1 tablespoon paprika

2 teaspoons ground cumin

2 teaspoons ground cardamom

1 teaspoon ground cloves

1 teaspoon sea salt

To serve (optional):

crispy poppadoms

tomato and cucumber salad

limes wedges

4–6 long, thin metal skewers

Serves 4–6

Chicken tandoori kebabs

As the name of this dish denotes, it should be cooked in a tandoori oven but, as most of us don't have such a wonderful invention at home, a charcoal grill is a good substitute. Some Indian and African cooks add red food dye to the marinade to obtain the reddish colouring associated with tandoori dishes.

To prepare the marinade, use a mortar and pestle, or an electric blender, to mince the chillies, garlic and ginger to a paste. Beat in the cream and oil with 3–4 tablespoons water to form a smooth mixture. Beat in the dried spices.

Place the chicken pieces in a bowl and rub with the marinade until thoroughly coated. Cover and chill in the refrigerator for about 48 hours. Lift the chicken pieces out of the marinade and thread them onto the skewers. Prepare a charcoal or conventional grill. Brush the chicken with the melted ghee and cook for 3–4 minutes. Serve with crispy poppadoms, a salad of finely diced tomato, cucumber and onion with fresh coriander, and wedges of lime for squeezing, if liked.

900 g chicken breasts, cut into
  bite-sized pieces

2 tablespoons ghee or butter,
  melted

For the marinade:

450 ml thick natural yoghurt,
  left to drain through muslin
  for 1–2 hours

40 g fresh ginger, peeled and
  pounded to a pulp

2–3 garlic cloves, crushed

2 teaspoons chilli powder

2 teaspoons ground cinnamon

2 teaspoons ground cumin

1 teaspoon ground coriander

1 teaspoon ground cardamom

1 teaspoon ground cloves

1 teaspoon ground black pepper

1–2 teaspoons salt

freshly squeezed juice of 1 lemon

For the minted yoghurt:

6 tablespoons thick natural yoghurt

freshly squeezed juice of ½ a lemon

2 garlic cloves, crushed

sea salt and freshly ground
  black pepper

leaves from a small bunch of fresh
  mint, finely chopped or shredded

*a packet of short wooden or
  bamboo skewers, soaked in
  water before use*

Serves 4–6

Gingery chicken tikka kebabs
with minted yoghurt

This version of the classic Indian tikka is incredibly versatile
as you can vary the spices according to your taste and you
can serve the tasty little bits of chicken with drinks, as a
snack tucked into pitta bread, or as part of barbecue spread.
It is delicious served with this refreshing minted yoghurt or
your favourite Indian chutney.

To prepare the marinade, beat together the strained yoghurt, ginger
and garlic then stir in the spices and lemon juice. Toss the chicken
pieces in the marinade, making sure they are thoroughly coated.
Cover, refrigerate and leave to marinate for at least 2 hours.

Meanwhile, prepare the minted yoghurt. Beat the yoghurt with the
lemon juice and garlic. Season to taste and stir in the mint.

Thread the chicken onto the prepared skewers, leaving behind any
excess marinade, and brush the melted ghee over them. Prepare
a charcoal or conventional grill. Cook the kebabs for about 3 minutes
on each side, until the chicken is nicely browned and cooked through.
Serve with the minted yoghurt on the side for dipping.

Spicy chicken kebabs
with ground almonds

700 g chicken breasts, cut into
   bite-sized pieces

freshly squeezed juice of 1 lemon

1 teaspoon sea salt

1–2 tablespoons peanut or
   sunflower oil

1 onion, halved and sliced

25 g fresh ginger, peeled and
   finely grated

2 garlic cloves, crushed

2–3 tablespoons ground almonds

1–2 teaspoons garam masala

125 ml thick double cream

To serve:

1–2 tablespoons butter

2–3 tablespoons blanched,
   flaked almonds

a small bunch of fresh flat leaf
   parsley, finely chopped

warmed flatbreads

4 long, thin metal skewers

Serves 4

In India, Turkey and North Africa, nuts are often used in recipes. Sometimes they are hidden in the minced meat of a kofta (meatball), or they form a coating on the meat. In this dish, the combination of ground almonds and browned onions in the marinade gives the meat a sweet, rich flavour.

First toss the chicken pieces in the lemon juice and salt to blanch them. Put aside for 15 minutes.

Meanwhile, heat the oil in a frying pan. Add the onion and cook until golden brown and crisp. Remove the onion from the oil and spread it out on a sheet of kitchen paper to drain and cool. Reserve the oil in the frying pan.

Using a mortar and pestle, or an electric blender, pound the onions to a paste and beat in the ginger and garlic. Add the almonds and garam masala and bind with the cream. Tip the almond and onion mixture over the chicken and mix well. Cover and leave in the refrigerator to marinate for about 6 hours.

Thread the chicken onto the skewers and brush them with the reserved onion oil. Prepare a charcoal or conventional grill. Cook the kebabs for 3–4 minutes on each side, until the chicken is nicely browned. Quickly melt the butter in a pan and stir in the flaked almonds until golden. Toss in the parsley and spoon the mixture over the grilled chicken. Serve hot with warmed flatbreads, if liked.

Duck satay with grilled pineapple and plum sauce

700 g duck breasts or boned thighs, sliced into thin, bite-sized strips

1–2 tablespoons peanut or coconut oil, for brushing

1 small pineapple, peeled, cored and sliced

Chinese plum sauce, to serve

For the marinade:

2–3 tablespoons light soy sauce

freshly squeezed juice of 1 lime

1–2 teaspoons sugar

1–2 garlic cloves, crushed

25 g fresh ginger, peeled and grated

1 small onion, grated

1–2 teaspoons ground coriander

1 teaspoon salt

a packet of wooden or bamboo skewers, soaked in water before use

Serves 4

Chicken satays are popular throughout Southeast Asia but in Vietnam, Cambodia and China, duck satays are common too. Duck is often served in the Chinese tradition of sweet and sour with a fruity sauce. You can buy ready-made bottled plum sauce in Chinese markets and most supermarkets.

To make the marinade, put the soy sauce and lime juice in a bowl with the sugar and mix until it dissolves. Add the garlic, ginger and grated onion and stir in the coriander and salt.

Place the strips of duck in a bowl and pour over the marinade. Toss well, cover and chill in the refrigerator for at least 4 hours. Thread the duck strips onto the skewers and brush them with oil.

Prepare a charcoal or conventional grill. Cook the satays for 3–4 minutes on each side, until the duck is nicely browned. Grill the slices of pineapple at the same time. When browned, cut them into bite-sized pieces and serve with the duck. Drizzle with the plum sauce to serve.

about 30 preserved vine leaves

4–5 large, skinless fillets of white fish, with all bones removed

For the marinade:

2–3 garlic cloves, crushed

1–2 teaspoons ground cumin

4 tablespoons olive oil

freshly squeezed juice of 1 lemon

1 teaspoon sea salt

For the tangy herb sauce:

50 ml white wine vinegar or freshly squeezed lemon juice

1–2 tablespoons sugar

a pinch of saffron threads

1 onion, finely chopped

2 garlic cloves, finely chopped

2–3 spring onions, finely sliced

a thumb-sized piece of fresh ginger, grated

2 fresh hot red or green chillies, finely sliced

a small bunch of fresh coriander, finely chopped

a small bunch of fresh mint, finely chopped

sea salt

a packet of short wooden or bamboo skewers, soaked in water before use

Serves 4

Vine-wrapped fish kebabs with tangy herb sauce

For these Mediterranean kebabs, almost any kind of firm, white fish fillet will do – monkfish or haddock work well. The fish is prepared in a simple marinade and then wrapped in the vine leaves, which become crisper with cooking.

First wash the vine leaves and soak them in several changes of water for 1 hour.

To prepare the marinade, mix all the ingredients together in a shallow bowl. Cut each fillet of fish into roughly 8 bite-sized pieces and coat in the marinade. Cover and chill in the refrigerator for 1 hour.

Meanwhile, prepare the tangy herb sauce. Put the vinegar in a small saucepan with the sugar and 1–2 tablespoons water. Heat until the sugar has dissolved. Bring to the boil for 1 minute, then leave to cool. Add the other ingredients, mix well and spoon it into small individual bowls.

Lay the prepared vine leaves on a flat surface and place a piece of marinated fish in the centre of each one. Fold the edges over the fish and wrap the leaf up into a small parcel. Push the parcels onto the individual skewers and brush with any remaining marinade.

Prepare a charcoal or conventional grill. Cook the kebabs for 2–3 minutes on each side. Serve immediately with a dish of tangy herb sauce on the side for dipping.

fish

Char-grilled tamarind prawns

500 g fresh, large prawns, deveined and trimmed of heads, feelers and legs

For the marinade:

3 tablespoons tamarind pulp*

250 ml warm water

2 tablespoons sweet soy sauce

1 tablespoon sugar

freshly ground black pepper

To serve:

leaves from a small bunch of fresh coriander

2–4 fresh green chillies, deseeded and sliced

a packet of wooden or bamboo skewers, soaked in water before use

Serves 2–4

This is popular street food in Malaysia and Indonesia. The aroma emanating from the stalls as the marinated prawns are grilled over charcoal, makes you feel very hungry.

Rinse the prepared prawns well, pat dry and using a very sharp knife, make an incision along the curve of the tail. Set aside.

Put the tamarind pulp in a bowl and add the warm water. Soak the pulp, until soft, squeezing it with your fingers to help dissolve it. Strain the liquid and discard any fibre or seeds. In a bowl, mix together the tamarind juice, soy sauce, sugar and black pepper. Pour it over the prawns, rubbing it over the shells and into the incision in the tails. Cover, refrigerate and leave to marinate for about 1 hour.

Insert a skewer into each marinated prawn. Prepare a charcoal or conventional grill. Cook the prawns for about 3 minutes on each side, until the prawn shells have turned orange, brushing them with the marinade as they cook. Serve immediately, garnished with the coriander leaves and chillies.

*Note Tamarind lends a rich, sweet-sour flavour to dishes. The tropical trees produce fresh pods that are either sold fresh or processed into pulp or paste for convenience and long shelf life. You may think you've never tried tamarind, however it is an essential ingredient in several traditional British condiments, most notably brown sauce. Look out for it in Caribbean markets – semi-dried tamarind pulp comes in soft rectangular blocks wrapped in plastic. The darker concentrated paste is sold in tubs and is a more processed product.

500 g boned swordfish, cut into
bite-sized chunks

2 oranges, cut into wedges

a handful of fresh bay leaves

2–3 teaspoons ground sumac*

For the marinade:

1 onion, grated

1–2 garlic cloves, crushed

freshly squeezed juice of ½ a lemon

2–3 tablespoons olive oil

1–2 teaspoons tomato purée

sea salt and freshly ground
black pepper

*4 metal skewers or 4–6 wooden
skewers, soaked in water
before use*

Serves 4

Swordfish kebabs
with oranges and sumac

Any firm-fleshed fish, such as tuna, trout, salmon, monkfish
and sea bass, can be used for these mighty Middle Eastern
kebabs. Make life easy and buy the swordfish ready boned
from the fishmonger. Exotic sumac adds a lemony tang.

In a shallow bowl, mix together the ingredients for the marinade. Toss
the chunks of swordfish in the marinade and set aside to marinate for
30 minutes.

Thread the marinated fish onto the skewers, alternating it with the
orange segments and the occasional bay leaf. If there is any marinade
left, brush it over the kebabs.

Prepare a charcoal or conventional grill. Cook the kebabs for
2–3 minutes on each side, until the fish is nicely browned. Sprinkle the
kebabs with sumac and serve.

*Note Sumac is an increasingly popular spice. It grows wild, but
is also cultivated in Italy, Sicily and throughout the Middle East. It is
widely used in Lebanese, Syrian, Turkish and Iranian cooking. The red
berries have an astringent quality, with a pleasing sour-fruit flavour. They
are used whole, but ground sumac is available from Middle Eastern
grocers or specialist online retailers.

Monkfish kebabs with chermoula

900 g monkfish tail, cut into chunks

12–16 cherry tomatoes

1–2 teaspoons smoked paprika

1–2 lemons, cut into wedges

For the chermoula:

2 garlic cloves

1 teaspoon coarse sea salt

1–2 teaspoons cumin seeds,
  crushed or ground

1 fresh red chilli, deseeded
  and chopped

freshly squeezed juice of 1 lemon

2 tablespoons olive oil

a small bunch of fresh coriander,
  roughly chopped

*4–6 metal skewers or 4–6 wooden
  skewers, soaked in water
  before use*

Serves 4–6

Chermoula is a classic Moroccan flavouring of garlic, chilli, cumin and fresh coriander, which is employed as a marinade for fish and chicken tagines and grilled dishes. Any meaty, white fish can be used for this recipe but monkfish cooks particularly well over charcoal.

To make the chermoula, use a mortar and pestle to pound the garlic with the salt to a smooth paste. Add the cumin, chilli, lemon juice and olive oil and stir in the coriander.

Place the fish chunks in a shallow dish and rub with the chermoula. Cover and chill in the refrigerator for 1–2 hours.

Thread the marinated monkfish and cherry tomatoes alternately onto the skewers. Prepare a charcoal or conventional grill. Cook the kebabs for about 2 minutes on each side, until the monkfish is nicely browned. Dust with a little paprika and serve with wedges of lemon for squeezing over them.

Stuffed char-grilled sardines

4 good-sized fresh sardines

2 tablespoons olive oil

4–6 spring onions, finely sliced

2–3 garlic cloves, crushed

1 teaspoon cumin seeds, crushed

1 teaspoon ground sumac
(see note on page 38)

1 tablespoon pine nuts

1 tablespoon currants, soaked
in warm water for 15 minutes
and drained

a small bunch of fresh flat leaf
parsley finely chopped

sea salt and freshly ground
black pepper

For basting:

3 tablespoons olive oil

freshly squeezed juice of 1 lemon

1–2 teaspoons ground sumac

*a packet of wooden skewers,
soaked in water before use*

Serves 4

This dish is best made with good-sized plump, fresh sardines, which are slit from head to tail with the back bone removed. Full of mediterranean flavours, this is a great recipe for outdoor cooking on the barbecue while enjoying the summer sunshine.

To prepare the sardines, remove the bone, gently massage the area around it to loosen it. Using your fingers, carefully prise out the bone, snapping it off at each end, while keeping the fish intact. Rinse the fish and pat it dry before stuffing.

Heat the oil in a heavy-based pan and stir in the spring onions until soft. Add the garlic, cumin and sumac. Stir in the pine nuts and pre-soaked currants, and fry until the pine nuts begin to turn golden. Toss in the parsley and season with salt and pepper. Leave to cool.

Place each sardine on a flat surface and spread the filling inside each one. Seal the fish by threading the skewers through the soft belly flaps.

Mix together the olive oil, lemon juice and sumac and brush some of it over the sardines. Prepare a charcoal or conventional grill. Cook the stuffed fish for 2–3 minutes on each side, basting them with the rest of the olive oil mixture. Serve immediately.

Peri-peri prawn satay

24 large tiger prawns, slit along
    the back bone to remove the vein
    and head
12 fresh lime or lemon leaves

For the peri-peri:
175 g butter
3–4 garlic cloves, crushed
100 ml olive oil
4 dried red chillies, left whole
freshly squeezed juice of 2 lemons
sea salt

*a packet of wooden or bamboo
    skewers, soaked in water
    before use*

Serves 4–6

Peri-peri is a chilli- and lemon-flavoured buttery oil used
for marinating chicken and fish and in East and West Africa.
A legacy of the Portuguese influence in the region, the oil
takes its name from the Portuguese word for bird's eye
chillies, peri-peri. This spicy satay makes a good starter.

To make the peri-peri, melt the butter in a frying pan and stir in
the garlic. Set aside. Heat the olive oil in a separate pan and add the
chillies. Turn off the heat and leave the oil to cool with the chillies still
in it. When cool, transfer the oil to a mixing bowl and beat in the
garlic-flavoured butter, lemon juice and a little salt.

Thread the prawns onto the prepared skewers, alternating them with
the lime or lemon leaves. Brush the prawns with the peri-peri butter.
Prepare a charcoal or conventional grill. Cook the satays for about
2 minutes on each side, basting them with the peri-peri, until the
prawn shells have turned orange. Serve immediately with any
remaining peri-peri on the side for dipping.

Prawn and scallop kebabs
with walnut sauce

12 large fresh prawns, shelled
to the tail

8 fresh scallops, shelled and
thoroughly cleaned

8 cherry tomatoes

1 green pepper, cut into
bite-sized squares

For the marinade:

freshly squeezed juice of 2 lemons

4 garlic cloves, crushed

1 teaspoon ground cumin

1 teaspoon paprika

sea salt

For the walnut sauce:

115 g shelled walnut halves

2 slices day-old bread, soaked
in water and squeezed dry

2–3 garlic cloves, crushed

3–4 tablespoons olive oil

freshly squeezed juice of 1 lemon

a dash of white wine vinegar

sea salt and freshly ground
black pepper

*a packet of wooden or bamboo
skewers, soaked in water
before use*

Serves 4

This is one of the most popular ways to enjoy the jumbo
prawns and scallops along the Mediterranean coast of Syria,
Turkey and Lebanon. Threaded onto skewers with peppers
and tomatoes, they are served with a garlicky walnut sauce.

To make the marinade, mix together the lemon juice, garlic, cumin,
paprika and a little salt in a bowl. Rub the mixture into the prawns and
scallops. Cover, refrigerate and leave to marinate for about 1 hour.

Meanwhile, prepare the walnut sauce. Using a mortar and pestle,
pound the walnuts to a paste, or whizz them in an electric blender.
Add the bread and garlic and pound to a paste. Drizzle in the olive oil,
stirring all the time, and beat in the lemon juice and vinegar. The sauce
should be smooth with the consistency of thick double cream – if it's
too dry, stir in a little water. Season the sauce with salt and pepper
and set aside.

Thread the prawns and scallops onto the skewers, alternating with
the tomatoes and green pepper, until all the ingredients are used
up. Prepare a charcoal or conventional grill. Cook the kebabs for
2 minutes on each side, basting with any of the leftover marinade, until
the prawn shells are orange, the scallops tender and the tomatoes
and peppers lightly browned. Serve hot with the walnut sauce on the
side for dipping.

vegetables

Summer vegetable kebabs with home-made pesto

2 aubergines, cut into chunks

2 courgettes, cut into chunks

2–3 peppers, stalks removed, deseeded and cut into chunks

12–16 cherry tomatoes

4 red onions, cut into quarters

For the marinade:

4 tablespoons olive oil

freshly squeezed juice of ½ a lemon

2 garlic cloves, crushed

1 teaspoon sea salt

For the pesto:

3–4 garlic cloves, roughly chopped

leaves from a large bunch of fresh basil (at least 30–40 leaves)

½ teaspoon sea salt

2–3 tablespoons pine nuts

extra virgin olive oil, as required

about 60 g freshly grated Parmesan

4–6 metal skewers or wooden skewers, soaked in water before use

Serves 4–6

Full of sunshine flavours, these kebabs can be served with couscous and a salad, or with pasta tossed in some of the pesto sauce. Home-made pesto is very personal – some people like it very garlicky, others prefer lots of basil or Parmesan – so simply adjust the quantities to suit your taste.

To make the pesto, use a mortar and pestle to pound the garlic with the basil leaves and salt – the salt will act as an abrasive and help to grind. (If you only have small mortar and pestle, you may have to do this in batches.) Add the pine nuts and pound them to a paste. Slowly drizzle in some olive oil and bind with the grated Parmesan. Continue to pound and grind with the pestle, adding in enough oil to make a smooth sauce. Set aside.

Put all the prepared vegetables in a bowl. Mix together the olive oil, lemon juice, garlic and salt and pour it over the vegetables. Using your hands, toss the vegetables gently in the marinade, then thread them onto the skewers.

Prepare a charcoal or conventional grill. Cook the kebabs for 2–3 minutes on each side, until the vegetables are nicely browned. Serve the kebabs with the pesto on the side for drizzling.

Spicy tofu satay
with soy dipping sauce

300 g tofu, rinsed, drained, patted
  dry and cut into bite-sized cubes

leaves from a small bunch of fresh
  basil, shredded, to serve

sesame oil, for frying

For the marinade:

3 lemongrass stalks, trimmed and
  finely chopped

1 tablespoon peanut oil

3 tablespoons soy sauce

1–2 fresh red chillies, deseeded
  and finely chopped

2 garlic cloves, crushed

1 teaspoon ground turmeric

2 teaspoons sugar

sea salt

For the soy dipping sauce:

4–5 tablespoons soy sauce

1–2 tablespoons Thai fish sauce

freshly squeezed juice of 1 lime

1–2 teaspoons sugar

1 fresh red chilli, deseeded and
  finely chopped

*a packet of wooden or bamboo
  skewers, soaked in water
  before use*

Serves 3–4

Here is a very tasty dish that does wonderful things to tofu, which can be rather bland. Full of the flavours of Southeast Asia, this Vietnamese dish is sold at street stalls as a snack but serve it as a starter or with noodles as a main dish.

To make the marinade, mix the lemongrass, peanut oil, soy sauce, chilli, garlic and turmeric with the sugar until it has dissolved. Add a little salt to taste and toss in the tofu, making sure it is well coated. Leave to marinate for 1 hour.

Prepare the soy dipping sauce by whisking all the ingredients together. Set aside until ready to serve.

To cook the tofu, you can stir-fry the cubes in a wok with a little sesame oil and then thread them onto sticks to serve, or you can skewer them and grill them over charcoal or under a conventional grill for 2–3 minutes on each side. Serve the tofu hot, garnished with the shredded basil and with the dipping sauce on the side.

Roasted pumpkin wedges
with lime and spices

1 medium-sized pumpkin, halved
  lengthways, deseeded, and cut
  into 6–8 segments

2 teaspoons coriander seeds

1 teaspoon cumin seeds

1 teaspoon fennel seeds

1–2 teaspoons ground cinnamon

2 dried red chillies, chopped

2 garlic cloves

2 tablespoons olive oil

coarse sea salt

finely grated zest of 1 lime

*6 wooden or metal skewers,
  to serve (optional)*

Serves 6

This is a great way to enjoy pumpkin. Serve these spicy wedges on their own or with any grilled, roasted or barbecued meat or poultry dish. Save the seeds and roast them lightly with a little oil and coarse salt as a nibble.

Preheat the oven to 200°C (400°F) Gas 6.

Using a mortar and pestle, grind all the dried spices with the salt. Add the garlic and a little of the olive oil to form a paste. Rub the mixture over the pumpkin wedges and place them, skin-side down, in a baking dish or roasting tray. Cook them in the preheated oven for 35–40 minutes, or until tender. Sprinkle over the lime zest and serve hot, threaded onto skewers, if using.

Pan-grilled aubergine
with honey and spices

8 aubergines, thickly sliced
  lengthways

olive oil, for brushing

2–3 cloves garlic, crushed

a thumb-sized piece of fresh
  ginger, peeled and crushed

1 teaspoon ground cumin

1 teaspoon harissa paste*

5 tablespoons runny honey

freshly squeezed juice of 1 lemon

sea salt

a small bunch of fresh flat leaf
  parsley, finely chopped

Buttery Couscous (see page 58),
  to serve

4 metal or wooden skewers,
  to serve (optional)

Serves 4

Hot, spicy, sweet and fruity are classic combinations of Moroccan cooking. In this delicious dish, these combinations send you on a thrilling journey. You can cook the aubergines in a ridged stove-top grill pan or under the grill.

Brush each aubergine slice with olive oil and cook them in a stove-top grill pan or grill them under a conventional grill, turning them over so that they are lightly browned.

In a wok or large heavy frying pan, fry the garlic in a little olive oil, then stir in the ginger, cumin, harissa, honey and lemon juice. Add a little water to thin it, then place the aubergine slices in the liquid and cook gently for about 10 minutes, until they have absorbed the sauce. Add more water if necessary and season to taste with salt.

Thread the aubergines onto the skewers, if using, and garnish with the parsley. Serve hot or at room temperature as meal on their own with couscous, or as an accompaniment to grilled meat.

*Note Harissa is a fiercely hot red chilli purée from North Africa, where it is used extensively as a condiment and diluted with stock, water or fresh tomato sauce to flavour couscous dishes, soups and tagines (stews). Moroccan food is growing in popularity so harissa paste is now widely available in larger supermarkets and from specialist on-line retailers.

350 g cauliflower florets

sunflower oil, for deep-frying

lime wedges, to serve

For the chutney:

1 onion, peeled and chopped

1–2 garlic cloves, peeled and chopped

leaves from a large bunch of fresh coriander

2–3 tablespoons freshly grated or desiccated coconut

1 teaspoon sugar

freshly squeezed juice of ½ a lemon

sea salt

For the batter:

150 g gram (chickpea) flour

2 teaspoons ground turmeric

1 teaspoon ground coriander

1 teaspoon ground fenugreek

1 teaspoon cayenne pepper or chilli powder

½ teaspoon bicarbonate of soda

1–2 teaspoons cumin seeds, crushed

sea salt and freshly ground black pepper

a packet of short wooden or bamboo skewers, to serve (optional)

Serves 4

Cauliflower fritter satay with coriander and coconut chutney

Indian in style, these cauliflower fritters are served as a satay snack with a local chutney, Indonesian sweet soy sauce or even tomato ketchup.

First prepare the coriander and coconut chutney. Using a pestle and mortar, or an electric blender, pound the onion with the garlic and salt. Add the coriander leaves and mix to a paste. Beat in the coconut, sugar and lemon juice and thin with a little water to form a smooth purée. Set aside.

Sift the gram flour with the ground spices and bicarbonate of soda into a bowl. Add the cumin seeds and seasoning and bind with enough water to form a thick batter.

Heat sufficient oil in a wok or large frying pan for deep-frying. Dip the cauliflower florets into the batter and drop them into the oil, working in batches, and cook until golden brown. Drain them on kitchen paper. Spear each cauliflower fritter with a skewer, if using, and serve hot with the coriander and coconut chutney on the side for dipping.

Buttery couscous

350 g couscous, rinsed and
  drained

400 ml warm water plus
  ½ teaspoon sea salt

2 tablespoons sunflower or olive oil

25 g butter, cut into small cubes

Serves 4–6

This is just a basic recipe to which you can add fresh herbs,
a spice paste or chopped nuts and dried fruits of your choice.

Preheat the oven to 180°C (350°F) Gas 4.

Tip the couscous into an ovenproof dish. Pour the salted water over
the couscous. Leave it to absorb the water for about 10 minutes.
Using your fingers, rub the oil into the grains to break up the lumps
and aerate them.

Scatter the butter over the surface and cover with a piece of foil or wet
greaseproof paper. Put in the preheated oven for 15 minutes to heat
through. Fluff up the grains with a fork before serving.

Bulghur with ghee

2 tablespoons ghee or
  1 tablespoon olive oil plus
  a knob of butter

2 onions, chopped

350 g bulghur (cracked wheat),
  thoroughly rinsed and drained

600 ml vegetable or chicken stock
  or water

sea salt and freshly ground
  black pepper

Serves 4–6

Bulghur is delicious served with most kebabs. You could add
diced carrots, peas, spices, nuts or herbs to this basic recipe.

Melt the ghee in a heavy-based saucepan. Add the onions and stir
until soft. Add the bulghur, tossing it thoroughly with the onions.

Pour in the stock, season and stir well. Bring to the boil and cook for
1–2 minutes, then reduce the heat and simmer, uncovered, until all the
liquid has been absorbed. Turn off the heat, cover the pan with a clean
tea towel, and press a lid on top. Leave to steam for a further 10–15
minutes, then fluff up with a fork before serving.

accompaniments

Rice pilaf

450 g long grain rice, rinsed and soaked in water for 30 minutes

1–2 tablespoons ghee or 1 tablespoon olive oil plus a knob of butter

1 onion, chopped

1 teaspoon sugar

4–6 cardamom pods, bashed to release flavour from the seeds

4 cloves

600 ml water plus 1 teaspoon sea salt

Serves 4–6

This recipe is the base to which other ingredients, such as nuts, ginger and coconut, can be added. Ground turmeric and saffron can also be added for fragrance and colour.

Heat the ghee in a heavy-based saucepan. Add the onion and sugar and fry until golden. Add the cardamom pods and cloves and stir in the pre-soaked rice, making sure the grains are coated in the ghee. Pour the salted water over the rice and bring to the boil.

Reduce the heat and simmer for 15–20 minutes, uncovered, until the liquid has been absorbed. Turn off the heat, cover the saucepan with a clean tea towel, followed by a lid, and leave the rice to steam for a further 10 minutes before fluffing up and serving.

Simple noodles
with ginger and chilli

225 g dried rice, wheat or egg noodles

1–2 tablespoons vegetable oil

25 g fresh ginger, peeled and shredded

1–2 fresh red chillies, deseeded and finely chopped

1–2 garlic cloves, finely chopped

3–4 tablespoons soy sauce

2–3 teaspoons runny honey

leaves from a small bunch of fresh coriander, finely chopped

Serves 4

These simple noodles are good served with satay dishes and can also form the base of a more creative dish with shredded cabbage, julienned carrot, beansprouts, tofu and peanuts.

Soak the noodles in water according to the packet instructions. Heat the oil in a wok or large frying pan. Add the ginger, chillies and garlic and stir-fry until fragrant and just beginning to colour. Toss in the reconstituted noodles and add the soy sauce and honey. Stir well. Toss in the chopped coriander and serve immediately.

Roasted sweet potato
with garlic and ginger

2–3 good-sized sweet potatoes, peeled and cut into chunks

a thumb-sized piece of fresh ginger, peeled and cut into thin strips

4–6 garlic cloves, smashed

3–4 tablespoons olive oil

sea salt and freshly ground black pepper

To serve (optional):

lemon wedges

thick natural yoghurt

Serves 4

Sweet potato is delicious roasted as the natural sugars caramelize in the oil and the softened flesh absorbs the flavours. The wedges are delicious served as a side dish with most meat, poultry or fish kebabs, or just enjoyed on their own with lemon wedges and creamy yoghurt.

Preheat the oven to 200°C (400°F) Gas 6.

Place the sweet potatoes in an ovenproof dish with the ginger and garlic. Pour in the olive oil, toss well, to coat the sweet potatoes and put them in the preheated oven for about 40 minutes, until the sweet potato is tender and slightly caramelized. Season to taste.

Serve the potato wedges as an accompaniment to kebabs or enjoy them on their own with lemon wedges for squeezing and a generous dollop of yoghurt.

Index